Crowning Glory

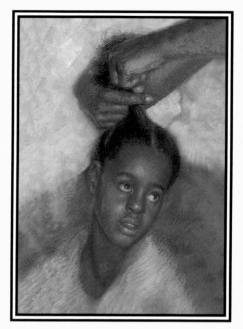

POEMS BY JOYCE CAROL THOMAS

ILLUSTRATED BY BRENDA JOYSMITH

JOANNA COTLER BOOKS

An Imprint of HarperCollinsPublishers

For Gloria Pecot,

with love

—JCT

In memory of my mother,

Ada Benton Smith

—BJ

Tenderness

I remember Mama

The hairdresser

And the way she hummed

When she plaited my hair.

"Mama," I asked,

"Is this my crowning glory?"

First Braids

My mother braids my hair

Stirring the roots

With knowing fingers

"This here is your glory,"

She says

I look in the mirror and see:

My dream me

Running in plaited loops

From the top

Of my head

On down

To the locks of my shoulders

Wavy

Mama has been working with the curling irons

Almost an hour

Turning straight into wavy

Until she has to stop and fan herself

The irons heat on the stove eye's flame

Turned just so high

When the curlers are so red they smoke

Mama picks them up again in her twirling hand

And my sister's hair stretches

Then curls back on itself

As steam rises from the hot irons

Their handles make that *click click clicking* sound

Sizzling flat into round

Great-Grandma's Way

"It has always been so,"

She says

Winding the thread

Through the hair on her head

"To make the hair strong

You can't go wrong

Using black twine, nothing's better

To wrap and keep loose ends together."

Locks

My cousin says she's waiting for

Her dreads to lock

And I wait too

It takes more than a minute or an hour

Days pass, then weeks

Months go by and I stop watching

Then one morning

My cousin has a twinkle in her eye

"Notice anything?" she asks

I say, "Glory be." I'm totally shocked

"Your hair is different

Your dreads have locked."

Mama's Glory

Mama says, "I wear my hair natural

In memory of a faraway place."

Her hair is thick and soft

A frame around her face

Her hair is a continent

Her glory on earth

"My Africa," she says

"Our ancestors' place of birth."

She picks it with a comb

'Til it stands sculptured and round

I like the way it looks and feels

A halo of a crown

Wearing Art

"Some days," says my aunt, "I just want colors."

She looks at a row of cloth

Cotton purples and checkered cocoa

Squares, rectangles

Triangles and strips

Carefully I pick a scarf

Ruby red and silk green

"Just right," she says

And wraps the cloth tightly

Around her head

It looks so perfect I can't imagine her without it

Adorned

Ribbons and combs

Feathers and beads

Bands and bows

Shells and nets

Flowers and hairpins

Rainbow barrettes

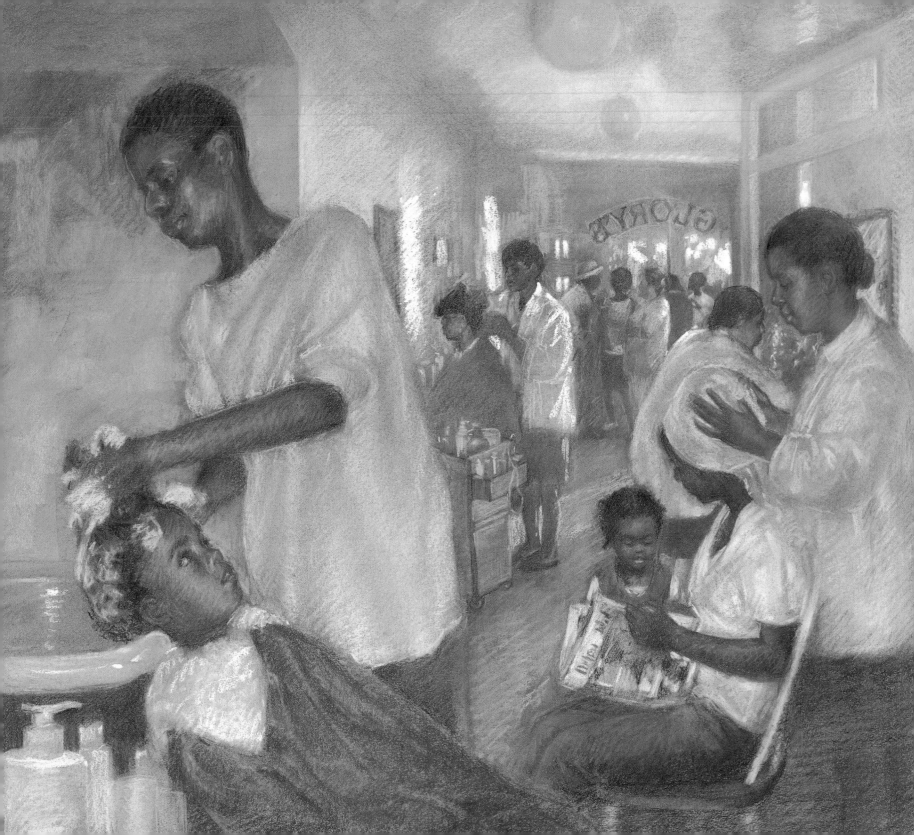

At Glory's Beauty Shop

At Glory's Beauty Shop

Warm water trickles over scalp

And mixes with thick suds

Cleansing my hair

I am so relaxed

I hardly have a care

Fingers massage my crown

As I hold my head back

Then spray rinses the shampoo

Until my hair is shiny black

"Sit up now," the hairdresser says

As she conditions the strands

Then towels dry

With vigorous hands

It feels so good

I wish she'd never stop

At Glory's Beauty Shop

Grandma's Helper

Sometimes my grandma

Wears a wig

It's rich with hair

And way too big

When I try to put it on

"Girl, what you doing?"

She says, leaning on her cane

"That's Grandma's helper

It's not that I'm vain."

"Can't get to the beauty shop sometimes

So I make do instead

I borrow somebody else's hair

And wear it on my head."

Glad Hats

Pink hats for the fashion parade

Hats ribboned and hats homemade

Hats bought from downtown stops

Hats picked from boutique shops

Green hats with flower rims

Hats made with skinny brims

Hats made of straw and linen

Hats made for girls and women

White hats on Mother's Day

Hats made the old-fashioned way

Hats for fishing 'til day is done

Hats to shade us from the sun

Red hats for baseball games

Hats for walking in the rain

Hats for driving in the winter

Hats for Grandma's Sunday dinner

Swimming Hair

I loosen my berets

I unribbon my ribbons

I take down my cornrows

And watch my acrobatic hair stand

All over my head all by itself

Now that I have undone my do

I dive into cool water

And wiggle through wet light

Left by the sweetest rain

With each stroke of my arms and legs

My hair collects beads, water jewels

My hair is ruled by its own ruly self and

Blessed by water's fingers

Good Hair

"What is good hair?"

I ask my daddy

And Mama answers, "Why it's understood,

Sister, if it's on your head it's good!"

Crowning Glory

hair

a gift

wrapped

ribboned

curled

tied

Author's Note

It's breathtaking! The artful way African-American girls adorn their hair.

A shimmering mirror of their souls. Hair! Braided, pressed, dreadlocked,

hot-curled, crowned with ribbons, and beaded with jewels of joy. Precious!

The poetry in *Crowning Glory* is a tribute to my beautician mother and all

her hairdressing foremothers. In honoring the beauty of black girls, I welcomed

the tenderhearted gifts of my own daughter and my seven beautiful grand-

daughters, who sat for these pastel portraits.

When I asked Brenda Joysmith to paint these poems more than ten

years ago, she answered, "Of course!" Now as I hug this book and travel its

pages, I salute the patience that art and life demand.

Crowning Glory Text copyright © 2002 by Joyce Carol Thomas Illustrations copyright © 2002 by Brenda Joysmith Printed in Hong Kong. All rights reserved. www.harperchildrens.com Library of Congress Cataloging-in-Publication Data Thomas, Joyce Carol. Crowning glory : poems / by Joyce Carol Thomas ; illustrated by Brenda Joysmith p. cm.   ISBN 0-06-023474-1 (lib. bdg.) —ISBN 0-06-023473-3 Summary: A collection of poems, including "First Braids," "Great-Grandma's Way," and "Mama's Glory," in which an Afro-American girl celebrates herself, her family, and her heritage. 1. Afro-American girls—Juvenile poetry. 2. Afro-American families—Juvenile poetry. 3. Afro-Americans—Juvenile poetry. 4. Girls—Juvenile poetry. 5. Family—Juvenile poetry. 6. Children's poetry, American. 7. Afro-Americans—Poetry. 8. Family—Poetry. 9. American poetry. PS3570.H565 C76 2002 96-26690 811'.54 dc—20 Typography by Alicia Mikles 1 2 3 4 5 6 7 8 9 10 ❖ First Edition